THE REA

THE R
EGYPTIAN DEAD

ACCORDING TO THE BELIEF OF
THE ANCIENT EGYPTIANS

First Edition 1902
A. Wiedemann

New Edition 2018
Edited by Tarl Warwick

COPYRIGHT AND DISCLAIMER

FOREWORD

This work, "The Realms of the Egyptian Dead", is a comprehensive if brief overview of some of the lore known about the pagan Egyptians and their conception of afterlife, rebirth, and related topics. Of interest here to the occultist, primarily, is its thorough bibliographic appendix as well as its reference to certain spells utilized by the Egyptians of far antiquity to overcome judgment or suffering and to ensure a modestly enjoyable afterlife- this of course symbolized within ritualism (which is now understood far better than in the days of the author, Wiedemann, although he does a thorough and largely accurate job here.) The symbols of course range from the use of small clay or similar figures thought to be able to be animated after death in order to serve the mummified Egyptian, to spells designed to navigate the afterlife itself on the way to the hoped-for final destination in what amounts to a vaguely Earthlike paradise of a primarily agricultural kind.

It should be noted (and is by the author) that different sub-groups of Egyptian lore are sometimes contradictory, especially from era to era- this is here explained in some detail, and is of great interest potentially for those who have chosen a pagan path and seek to emulate this particular "religion" (for it is more a compendium of different cults as we may term them, as Wiedemann points out.)

This edition of "Realms" has been carefully edited for format and some antiquated language has been modernized. Care has been taken to retain the original intent and meaning of all passages.

REALMS OF THE EGYPTIAN DEAD

In any attempt to form some concept of the world and human life, the question which has most keenly exercised both the peoples of antiquity and those of today is always the same; whence are the universe and its inhabitants, and whither does it all tend ? In the following pages we shall consider the ideas developed in the Nile Valley respecting the issue of all things, and especially concerning the death of man, and that other world to which after death he hoped or feared to go. It must, in the first place, be noted that in Egyptian texts no indications of the existence of any myth predicting the final destruction of the world have hitherto been found. Whether no such myth existed and men in the Nile Valley were unable to imagine that this best of all worlds should one day no longer be, or whether the absence of such indications is the result of chance cannot now be decided. The idea that men must logically have conceived an end of the world having accepted a beginning, a creation, does not apply to the Egyptians, who in their speculations disdained the claims of logic, accuracy and similar exactions of later times. But though they did not conceive the destruction of the whole world, they possessed myths which tell of attempts on the part of the gods- never entirely successful- to destroy portions of the earth, or rather mankind. As far as their contents are concerned, these myths belong to the widespread cycle of Deluge legends.

First to be noted in this connection is a passage in a hymn of about 1200 B.C. addressed to the deity embracing and ruling the whole world. It alludes to a deluge in the words: "Thy flood (the god's) rises to the heavens, and the roaring water of thy mouth is in the clouds. Thy jackals are on the mountains."

That is to say, the jackals, which, according to an idea

4

prevailing especially in the New Kingdom, drew the Sun-god in his boat, have retreated to the mountains. "The water of the god Horus covers the great spaces of all lands; the flood of waters covers all quarters of the heaven and the sea. The lands would be (even now) the dominion of the flood were they not under thy sway. The waters move now upon the way that thou appointest; they cannot pass over what thou ordainest (the path) that thou openest before them."

According to the text, this deluge which covered the trees and drove the Sun-god to the mountains came up from beneath, as the Egyptians supposed to be the case with the Nile flood. A similar story was probably at the source of the Platonic dialogue 'Timaeus,' in which Egyptian authorities are often quoted. There it is used as an argument to deny the flooding of the world and the destruction of its inhabitants- so far, at least, as Egypt is concerned. For, according to Plato, it was by similar floods in other lands that towns perished, and only the herdsmen were saved ; in Egypt, however, neither then nor at any other time did water flow down from above upon the fields; it came up from below, and hence it was that in Egypt were preserved the memorials of ancient times.

In the valley of the Nile the whole conception of a flood no doubt arose from the frequent occurrence of fossil shells in the strips of desert at the edge of the cultivated land and on the Egyptian hills. The Greeks also observed them, and it was on the fact of their presence that Herodotus based his theory of the origin of Egypt. He pronounced the land to be alluvial, formed by the gradual deposit of mud in an arm of the sea. This opinion is substantially correct, although the Greek historian greatly underestimated the time in which the process could have been completed, allowing only from ten to twenty thousand years.

The words immediately preceding the passage in Plato

alluded to above have often been adduced to prove that the tradition of a world conflagration had a place in Egyptian mythology.

But the passage in question by no means proves this. A priest of the city of Sais, in Lower Egypt, is there represented as saying that, in consequence of the divergence at long intervals of the heavenly bodies that encircle the earth, all that is on earth is destroyed by fire, but that the Nile protects the Egyptians by pouring forth its waters in flood.

According to this text, the destruction wrought by such a conflagration is denied as respects the Nile Valley. No more is to be made of certain passages in Egyptian writings which have been claimed as indicating the same myth. In them we read of a fire which threatened the god Horus, the son of Isis, and which Isis succeeded in extinguishing with water. This has been supposed to be a general conflagration, for the quenching of which the goddess caused water to rise. But in this passage there is no mention of a burning world; only of the burning of the place where Horus was at the time- probably the hut in the Delta where Isis hid him when she was seeking the body of Osiris, and where he was exposed to many dangers. The primitive means whereby Isis procured the water for the extinction of a world in flames were at least somewhat peculiarly inadequate for the purpose; an early version of this ingenuous passage is found in the Ebers papyrus (about 1800 B.C.).

Thus, regarding the destruction of the world whether by water or by fire, there is nothing in Egyptian texts to throw light on such ideas in other countries. We are much more fully informed concerning a tradition which relates to a divine attempt to exterminate the sinful race of mankind. This myth has been preserved in two versions in the graves of Kings Seti I. and Rameses III., and in these forms dates therefore from about 1400 to 1200 b.c. Several other references to it exist, showing that from the second millennium b.c. it must have been well known in Egypt. Whether it existed earlier it is impossible to say, no certain proofs of this having yet been discovered.

Like most Egyptian myths, this also is connected with the Sun-god Ra-Harmakhis, the first divine king of Egypt, whom the legends represent as entirely human. He grows old and weak like other men, and we read of him often as an old man from whose failing hands the reins of government are gradually slipping. Gods and men venture to resist him, trying to cast him from his throne or to push him more and more into the background. The myth now under consideration begins with these words:

"Ra is the god who created himself. He was the king of gods and men. Men took counsel together against his majesty and said, 'Lo! the god Ra is grown old; his bones have changed into silver, his limbs into gold, and his hair into lapis-lazuli.' "

The Sun-god heard these words and called together the other gods to consider what ought to be done to those men who owed their existence to the Eye, that is to say, to the tears of the god, and who now were rebelling against their lord and creator. The gods advised him to send out his Eye against the rebels in the form of the goddess Hathor-Sekhet- that is to say, an incarnation of the sun in his burning and scorching might. This was done. The goddess set forth to slay mankind. Several nights she waded in human blood from Heracleopolis Magna, in Middle Egypt, to Heliopolis, the most sacred city of the Nile Valley, where the gods were wont to meet in council. But mankind was not entirely exterminated, for the god soon repented him of his command. He sent messengers to Elephantine to fetch fruits to which an intoxicating and narcotic effect was ascribed. In Heliopolis these were pressed, and at the same time corn was crushed for beer; then the two were mixed and seven thousand jugs of beer made. During the night this beer was poured out over the fields which were covered with the blood of the men killed by Sekhet. "And the goddess Sekhet came in the morning; she found the fields flooded, she rejoiced, her heart was light, she went about drunken and no longer heeded men."

Mankind was saved; and in memory of this a feast was instituted at which much beer was drunk in honor of Sekhet, a feast that was celebrated up to the Greek period. But the god Ra was no longer willing to rule over ungrateful men. When men knew this they repented; they took bows and arrows and killed all who had rebelled against the god. Then Ra spoke: "Your sin is forgiven; the killing (you have done on my behalf) atones for the killing (my foes plotted against me)." In spite of this forgiveness, men so far failed of their aim that the old god held to his resolve to go away to a better world, newly created by himself. To earth he left as a substitute for his own sun-power a new young sun as lord and king.

These are the only indications to be found in Egyptian texts of the conception of an impending or once threatened destruction of the world and of mankind. Much fuller in every respect is the material that has been preserved relating to the Egyptian conception of the end of the individual, not only of the human individual- which must first be considered- but also of that of each god and animal as conceived on similar lines. It is owing to the peculiar character of the remains in the Nile Valley that we are so well informed on this point. These relics relate almost exclusively to death, and are the spoils of tombs and of funerary temples. Moreover, the thoughts of the Egyptians dwelt much and gladly on death, which had no particular terror for them any more than for modern Orientals. To them death was no final end, but only an interruption of their existence. It was a violent interruption certainly, for to the ancient Egyptian death was not a natural result of the wearing out of the body. To him each death was a kind of murder. The body of man throughout life was regarded as a battlefield where good and evil spirits fought for the mastery. If the man remained in health, the former had the upper hand; did he fall sick, the latter had succeeded in gaining ascendance; hence he must do his best to help the good spirits.

This he did by wearing amulets to drive away the evil ones, or by repeating spells against them. Even in diseases caused by evil spirits these were the orthodox remedies; the medicines administered at the same time only served to reduce symptoms and owed much of their virtue to spells repeated during their preparation. The cure was not due to the medicines, but to the conquest by spells and powerful magic symbols of the demon who had entered into the man and caused his suffering. With the departure of the demon the sickness ended.

The strife in and about the human body lasted a longer or a shorter time according to the power of the spirits at strife. But experience had taught men that in the end the evil spirits always won a species of victory. One of the countless male and female sicknesses, male and female deaths, as the Egyptians expressed it, succeeded at last in destroying the man's mortal frame. But this death of the body was only an incident in the struggle which lasted beyond the grave, and the existence of the immortal parts of the man might be threatened by many dangers even as his mortal frame had been exposed to risks during his lifetime. Hostile spirits could prepare for him a second death, and hence the Egyptian strove eagerly to find means which would be efficacious beyond the grave to protect from foes himself and his forefathers. Both in this world and the next, the best, and indeed the only hopeful precautionary measure against any threatened danger, was the knowledge of the appropriate spell. Egyptian religious literature, therefore, consists to a large extent of collections of such spells- they were sculptured on the walls of the grave or on the sides of the sarcophagus, or written on papyrus rolls and placed with the dead in the tomb.

Probably that is also the reason why there is so comparatively little to be learned from these religious texts regarding the actual conditions of existence in the world to come. They tell us exactly what name a man had to give when he arrived at one of the gates of eternity, exactly what the bench, helm, and sails of the death-ship were called; the exact forms of the many names and titles of Osiris, in what words the demons must be greeted who dwelt in the various areas of this mysterious kingdom; but they give no complete picture of the appearance of that world. It is certainly possible to translate the individual formulas but often impossible to understand them, as they refer to myths unknown to us, and this in a manner so far from clear that the myths cannot be reconstructed from the formulas. Here, for example, is a spell against snakes of about 3000B.C.:

"The snake curls round the calf; the snake curls round the calf, oh hippopotamus that earnest forth from the earth! Thou devouredst what came forth from thee. Snake, as thou descendest, lie down, draw back. The god Henpesetet is in the water, the snake is overthrown, thou seest the god Ra." What is meant by the calf, the hippopotamus and the snake, and in connection with what incident they come together, is not told.

The sentences give us words, but the meaning evades us. It is the same with countless other formulas of a similar kind, and this fact, together with the many clerical blunders committed by the early copyists in putting together their papyri, shows that even to them the spells were often not entirely comprehensible. To the difficulty caused by insufficiency of material in any restoration of the conception of a future life in the Nile Valley we must add a second; the entire absence of systematic thought that characterized the Egyptians and which permitted them to write and to believe the most contradictory doctrines at one and the same time. They never made any attempt to put their own religion into systematic form, to reject what was contradictory to the main dogmas and to make these consistent with one another. On the other and, they faithfully retained all that their ancestors had once believed, together with all that later generations had added, untroubled by the various modes of thought that existed side by side and mingled together. In this religious conglomerate the people received first all the various local cults which, arising from a common basis, had in different city and village temples gradually attained an independent and often very peculiar development. There remained also the ancient faiths in their original forms as once held among the various tribes from which the Egyptian people had sprung in primitive times, so that primitive Semitic, primitive Libyan and many other conceptions present themselves side by side in bewildering variety. Nor is this all. Within historic times many systems of religious thought were borrowed from neighboring nations and added without modification to the Egyptian stock, so that the Semitic Baal and Astarte, together with their companion deities, found equally accredited places alongside the native gods of Egypt.

It was long believed that this confusion of religious ideas was to be found in later texts only. Since the inscriptions in the pyramids of the Fifth and Sixth Dynasties have come to light we know that this chaos is as old as any literary Egyptian tradition. No doubt it must have come about gradually, but the period of its development lies beyond our knowledge of the Egyptian people. Hence it seems useless to indulge in hypotheses regarding its course which may be shattered by any stroke of a spade, any new discovery of a text. In the present state of our knowledge a cautious student will confine himself to stating the separate dogmas, examining their changes during Egyptian history and inquiring into their meaning. The question of their origin and of their age is better left on one side.

Among the various Egyptian conceptions of the other world one of the most important and most widely diffused is connected with the sun and its apparent course during the twenty-four hours. The traveling of the star of day was accomplished, in the opinion of the Egyptian, in exactly the same way as his own when he undertook a journey through his native land- namely, by boat. But the Sun-god traveled on a celestial ocean or a celestial Nile, flowing in a fairly straight course through the celestial land, as the earthly river flows through Egypt. On this river the sun-boat usually floated with the stream, so that it needed a rudder only; oars and sails are seldom named.

Only in exceptional cases is there any mention of a towing of the sun-boat, and then it is generally done by jackals. This recalls the manner in which boats were taken up stream in the Nile Valley, but the human force used here below was replaced in celestial regions by that of creatures partaking of the divine nature. In the middle of the sun-boat there is a shrine-like cabin, in which the Sun-god, represented by day as a hawk-headed man, stands or sits, and on the boat there is generally a helmsman, besides various gods forming the court of the king of heaven. According to the most numerous and the most ancient representations, the god uses for his journey during the daytime two boats, one for the morning, another for the afternoon, and changed boats at noon. In later times the journey was less simple. At the end of each hour the god disembarked and embarked again in another boat. The journey was supposed to occupy twelve hours; that is to say, the time from sunrise to sunset, divided into twelve equal parts. From this it may be concluded that for the Egyptian an hour was not a fixed space of time as it is with us. Its length varied with the season, being longest at midsummer, shortest at midwinter. The length of the hours of the night varied correspondingly. The time from sunset to sunrise was divided into twelve equal parts, and the variation in their length was, of course, the reverse of the variation in the hours of the day. Each hour was in charge of a special goddess, who throughout its duration kept watch and accompanied the Sun-god on that part of his voyage.

The day journey ended in the west- then began the night journey. The sun-boat floated back to sunrise in the east on a stream flowing through the kingdom of night. This journey of the Sun god seemed to the Egyptian symbolic of the life of man. The Sun god is born in the morning, ages in the course of the day, sinks in the evening as an old man into darkness to rise in the morning once more to new life. According to the general idea the birth and death of the Sun god took place daily. Elsewhere we have a second conception, according to which the process was completed in the course of a year. The god awakes with the spring sun to new life, and he dies with the sun of winter. Here the condition of death involved in the course of twenty-four hours is absent, or is reduced to a very short space of time. Judging from occasional allusions in the texts, there seem also to have been other conceptions according to which the life of the Sun-god was much longer, lasting three hundred and sixty five years or more, and which probably referred to chronological periods. But such indications are by no means clear, and it is certain that these ideas never attained any wide popularity.

An exhaustive description of the night journey of the Sun-god is first found in texts of the New Kingdom, i.e., after 1700 b.c., yet many passages in older inscriptions and pictorial representations, specially on coffins of the Middle Kingdom, indicate that the doctrine existed much earlier, though it does not seem to have taken fixed form until the second millennium. We have it in the Book of Am-Duat; i.e: "Of that which is in the Under-world"- and in the Book of the Gates, each of which describes independently the topography of the under-world. These texts are found in papyri and on sarcophagi, and more or less fully in the Tombs of the Kings from the Eighteenth to the Twentieth Dynasty, in a short as well as in a fuller and illustrated edition. In spite of the contradictory nature of their contents the Book of Am-Duat and the Book of the Gates are found inscribed in the same tomb; another indication how little attempt the Egyptians made at systematic thought on religious subjects.

These doctrines flourished at a time corresponding to a period of Egyptian history when the kings resided chiefly at Thebes, and they appear to have received much of their development in the circle of the Theban priesthood, for it is in the tombs of these priests and of their relatives that they have been found in writing. This fact also explains why the Sun-god of night is always represented in these books as a ramheaded man, since it was in the form of a ram that Amon, the great god of Thebes, had descended to earth. In this series of texts the ram's horns of the god are invariably represented as projecting from the sides of the head. Now it has been thought possible to prove that of the two kinds of rams associated with Egyptian deities, the ram with the horizontal horns was sacred to the god Chnuphis of Elephantine, and that the horn curling round the ear, so well known from the Roman statues of Jupiter Ammon, belonged to the god Amon. Figures of kings of the Nineteenth Dynasty wear such horns occasionally as a headdress in token of their descent from the god Anion, and with similar implication Alexander the Great and his successors had them sculptured on their statues. If this distinction applied all over Egypt it would lead to the repudiation of any connection between the nocturnal Sun-god and Anion of Thebes; but in face of the monuments such a theory would not hold good. In the period now under consideration, Amon is frequently represented with horizontal horns, even in circumstances where there can be no thought of a blending of his form with that of Chnuphis. It seems to have

14

been for the most part artistic or practical reasons which then decided the choice, and in statues the horizontal horns are almost always avoided as having the less durable form.

Over the entrances to the Tombs of the Kings there is carved as a kind of superscription a sun's disc, in which is placed the figure of the god as just described, and behind it is the figure of a large scarab. The first is the god of the Night Sun, to whose kingdom the tomb belonged, and whose dominions its inscriptions describe, while the scarab is an emblem of the Morning Sun wakening to new life, and is at the same time a symbol of the renewed life of man after his earthly death.

The order of the scenes in these representations of the under-world is generally the same. The reliefs run along the walls in three rows, one above another. The middle one shows the river of the under-world on which the sun-boat sails, sometimes carried along by the stream, sometimes by spells, and sometimes towed by spirits subject to the god. Above and below are pictures of the banks of the river. Ahead of the boat and on the banks stand, sit and lie, in bewildering variety, the innumerable demons that people the fields of the night. Sometimes they appear in human form, sometimes as animals, especially as snakes, whose presence was naturally to be expected in an underground kingdom. Sometimes they appear as cynocephali, which in the Nile Valley were often associated with the sun. Sometimes they are creatures half-animal, half-human, most grotesquely composite. The names of the demons as well as their pictures are given on the monuments, and thus we recognize that but few of them had any connection with the great gods of the land. Most of them are gods of one special function whose names indicate their immediate employment: "The Cutting One,", "The Rending One," "The Stabber." Some were friendly to the Sun-god, but countless others were hostile to him.

THE REALMS OF THE EGYPTIAN DEAD

At the head of the latter was the great snake Apopis, the incarnation of the power of darkness, who strives to bar the way of the Sun god and to work his destruction. At the last moment he is always conquered by the friends of the Sun god, fettered, cut asunder, but never finally killed. No matter how wounded, invariably he returns to life again, and resumes the strife with the good god of warmth and light, a strife which, in Egyptian opinion, never ended in victory on either side.

We need not here describe all the genii of this under-world. The various spirits, variously represented, may be studied in the two books to which we have referred above. The one text is easily distinguished from the other, for in the Book of Am-Duat each Hour-Space is separated from the next by a door; in the Book of the Gates the door is replaced by a fortified pylon. The demons, excepting a few companions of the Sun-god, always remain in the same Space, and according to this special doctrine of a future life, so do the men who have died. They join the Sun on his journey from the western horizon, and are left by the god in different parts of the underworld, where he gives them fields to till on which they must henceforth live as vassals, always ready to help their lord against his foes if any should threaten to attack him on his passage. Theirs, however, was no joyful lot. With delight they hailed the Sun-god on his appearance; but at the end of an hour he vanished, the door of their room closed after him, and for the next twenty three hours they had to wait in a darkness which was relieved only by the light which came from fire-breathing serpents, or from the sea of flame in which the captive foes of the Sun-god were burning. It is noticeable that the same fate overtakes high and low, kings and subjects. Few indeed are the mortals who succeed in escaping it, and those who do are not such as have lived good lives on earth; they are those who have acquired an exceptionally large knowledge of magic, and who have striven also never to show themselves enemies of the Sun-god. These succeeded in constraining him not to set them down on his course, but to bear them along in his train, ever circling round the heavens in the solar bark.

This view that good and bad were on the same footing as regards the life to come, and that the deity caused no special reward after death to fall to the lot of those who had obeyed his commands on earth, occasionally struck the ancient Egyptian as unjust. Hence there was introduced into the Book of the Gates a judgment scene- in which sentence is pronounced on the deceased- similar to that of the judgment before Osiris in the Book of the Dead, to which we shall presently recur. Between the fifth and the sixth Hour-Space there is a hall in which Osiris sits upon his throne, surrounded by the gods of his circle. In his presence the soul of the man is weighed against his deeds, while at the same time a cynocephalus, the animal incarnation of the god Thoth, drives from the hall with a stick a hog, the representative of Set, the god of evil, and banishes it from the company of the good. In the next Space the good are seen tilling the fields, while the wicked, tied to stakes, are awaiting their punishment and will eventually be cast into seas of water or fire. It is noticeable how little attempt has been made to work this judgment scene into the fabric of the rest of the text. It is inserted bodily to fill up a mental hiatus, and no trouble has been taken to alter those parts of the work which take it for granted that there is no such judgment.

Most significant of the trifling expenditure of thought that must have been given to it is the fact that the interpolation is not made at the beginning of the text, but much later on; logically, the judgment ought to take place before the god; accompanied by the dead, starts on his way through the under-world. Neither did the Egyptians ever attempt to represent in detail the journey of the souls of the just and the unjust as far as this judgment hall.

THE REALMS OF THE EGYPTIAN DEAD

The same melancholy conception of existence after death is to be noted in a series of exhortations to the enjoyment of life. From about 2000 b.c. these are found in many Egyptian texts, expressed in very various terms, but always alike in thought. For example, a stela puts into the mouth of a dead wife the following adjuration to her husband:

"Oh my comrade, my husband! Cease not to eat and drink, to be drunken, to enjoy the love of women, to hold festival. Follow thy longings by day and night. Give care no room in thy heart. For the West land (a domain of the dead) is a land of sleep and darkness, a dwelling place wherein those who are there remain. They sleep in their mummy forms, they wake no more to see their comrades, they see neither father nor mother, their heart does not yearn for wife and children. On earth each drinks the water of life, but I suffer with thirst. Water comes to him that sojourns on earth, but I pine for the water that is by me. I long for the breeze on the bank of the river to soothe my heart in its woe. For the name of the god who rules here is 'Total Death.' At his call all men come unto him, trembling with fear. He makes no difference between gods and men; in his eyes high and low are equal. He shows no favor to him who loves him; he carries away the child from his mother and the gray-haired man alike. None comes to worship him, for he is not gracious to his worshipers, and he pays no heed to him who brings gifts to him."

The systems hitherto considered all placed the dwelling of the dead in a kingdom below ground. Another series represents it as in the sky above the earth. Contradictory opinions reigned as to how the soul succeeded in gaining admission either to the sun-boat, or among the stars, or to the wide-spreading fields of the blessed. According to one theory the soul repaired to that spot on the horizon where the sun sank through a narrow cleft in a rock, and there clambered into the boat. We have seen already that, according to one view, with the help of magic the dead might succeed in sailing with the sun through the whole realm of the under-world, and in the morning rise with him again in the eastern sky. Others postulated the existence of a certain ladder, by means of which the dead could climb into heaven with the help of a particular spell. A third conception, connected with the practice of burning the body, represents the soul of the dead man as rising to heaven from his ashes. This idea, though very ancient in Egypt, never prevailed widely in historic times, for the burning of the body, which even at the beginning of Egyptian history had become rare, so as to be practiced occasionally only, and almost exclusively in the case of kings, was in later times superseded by embalming. The practice was not, however, forgotten, and traces of it are found in the second millennium B.C. in sacrifice offered at the burial of distinguished persons, when human beings were burned in order that they might be sent as quickly as possible after the dead man to act as his servants. The idea that burning was an efficacious method of forwarding anything to the dead continuously survived in the practice of dispatching gifts to the upper regions by means of burnt offerings, a custom in radical contrast to the far commoner one of placing them in the grave. The latter method presupposes at least a temporary sojourn of the dead man in the tomb.

A much more prevalent idea than either of these as to the means of transit from this world into the next was one according to which the soul rises to heaven in the form of a bird, in the case of a king almost invariably as a sparrowhawk. Usually, however, and especially where ordinary mortals were concerned, the soul took the form of the so-called ba, a human-headed bird, sometimes represented with human arms. Generally it was a male bird, it being an Egyptian idiosyncrasy to think of a deceased person in the next world as male, even though she were a woman, to call her "Osiris," and to attribute to her a male soul-bird. Seldom in early, though somewhat oftener in later, times, the dead woman keeps her sex, is called as an immortal not "Osiris" but "Hathor," and is figured as a soul-bird with a woman's headdress, without beard, and occasionally with a woman's breast.

Heaven once attained, the soul dwelt henceforth in the circle of the gods. The texts do not, as a rule, tell us how and on what principle a place was assigned to it, and what was its position in relation to the gods and to other souls that preceded and followed it thither. The pyramid inscriptions, which are of about 3000 B.C., are somewhat more detailed respecting the souls of the kings, and show that the king had first to win in fight with the older gods the place that he claimed as corresponding to his earthly rank. As it had been with the dead god Osiris when he was about to become king of the realm of the dead in the West, so was it exactly with the deceased Pharaoh. The old gods who had hitherto ruled there resisted the new dominion and must needs be conquered by force before the reign of Osiris could begin.

The arrival of the dead prince in heaven is described as follows:

"The sky weeps, the stars quiver, the warders of the gods tremble and their servants flee when they see the king arise as a spirit, as a god who lives on his fathers and takes possession of his mothers. His servants have caught the gods with a lasso, have found them good and dragged them forward, bound them, cut their throats and taken out their entrails, have cut them in pieces and boiled them in hot cauldrons. The king devours their magic power and eats their souls. The great gods are his breakfast, the medium gods his midday meal, the lesser gods his supper, and the old gods and goddesses he uses as fuel. The king devours every thing that comes in his way. He swallows all greedily, and his magic power becomes greater than all magic. He is an inheritor of might more than all other inheritors; he becomes the lord of heaven, for he ate all the crowns and all the arm-bands, he ate the wisdom of every god..." etc. By conquering and devouring the gods together with the emblems of their power and their ornaments, the king becomes lord of heaven. The idea that man can procure for himself spiritual qualities by purely material processes is widely diffused. The eating to this end of the heart and the brain of the conquered foe, or of a powerful animal, and other similar customs, are found among various peoples. In Egypt this train of thought was supported by much assertion. He who would be true ate truth in the form of a little image of the goddess of Truth. A god bestowed life and power by allowing his favored one to breathe in through his nostrils life and power in the form of the hieroglyphic signs representing them.

Immortality could be gained by sucking the breast of a goddess and imbibing her immortality with her milk. Thus, in the pyramid text, the king becomes all-embracing godhead by means of his meal of gods, though the fact must be emphasized that the other gods were not therefore supposed to cease to exist. As Truth may be eaten by an individual man and nevertheless endure to be consumed in the same way by others after him, so, in spite of having been devoured, the gods retained their independent existences. There is no indication as to how the Egyptians explained it that the king who had become a god kept his dominion and did not fall a victim to the next dead Pharaoh, who likewise was equipped with all magic power. Probably they did not trouble themselves about it, and were content to picture their own future life as pleasantly as possible without considering later generations and their claims on immortality.

Under the earth, as well as above it, the Egyptian imagined a realm of the dead; and he also held that on the earth itself a similar kingdom existed. The manner in which this resurrection on earth was supposed to be brought about is again very variously represented. Some of the conceptions are borrowed from plant life. From the body, or some part of it, such as a drop of blood shed by the dying man, there sprang up a tree which became his new body. Sometimes the seat of life was the blossom, sometimes the wood, so that if the tree were felled a splinter sufficed to prolong the life in question. This tree representing the living being after death became in later times, when the myths had lost their original force, the tree that overshadowed the chest containing the corpse of Osiris, the story of which is known to us through Greek authors. Other representations show, not a tree, but corn as springing from the body. According to widely diffused ideas, it was thus that Osiris woke to new life; and his example was, in a certain sense, catching. Sometimes there was placed near the coffin a bed on which a miniature cornfield in the form of Osiris was made to sprout in the hope that the deceased would follow the divine example.

To the Egyptian of historic times the sprouting was no symbol; the texts declare distinctly that "Osiris" was the corn that had sprung forth from his mummy. Owing to a similar train of thought, a conventionalized aquatic plant became one of the commonest amulets denoting the resurrection; and the goddesses, who are ever renewing their youth, carry the same as a scepter. Another series of accounts represents the resurrection as an awakening to new life of the body that has been laid in the grave. They tell in great detail, and often with an effect of much triviality, how the dead man opens his mouth again, how he can move his arms and legs, how his digestion begins to work and his power of generation returns to him. These various lines of thought can be grouped together as dealing with the doctrine of immortality in connection with Osiris. Much as they differ in detail they have this in common, that they always name the god Osiris as a prototype, as the first being to whose lot such a resurrection fell.

THE REALMS OF THE EGYPTIAN DEAD

Osiris, the son of the god of earth and the goddess of heaven, was the first king who ruled Egypt in human fashion; he showed his divine nature by his graciousness and beneficence. But he did not succeed in winning all hearts. His own brother Set plotted against him; with the aid of several other conspirators he ensnared Osiris and murdered him. According to the later form of this myth, the body of Osiris was placed whole in a chest and thrown into the Nile. It was found after long wanderings by his wife and sister the goddess Isis, the divine ideal to the Egyptians of wife and mother. According to an older legend, the murderers cut the body in pieces and scattered them over the land. For a long time Isis wandered up and down till she had found all, or almost all, the parts. She then put them together and restored the body in order to bury it. Other authorities, however, represent that each part was left on the spot where it was found, and buried in one of the temples that the Greeks afterwards distinguished by the name of "Serapeum." In such sanctuaries special respect was paid to certain parts of the god's body; for example, in Letopolis the neck, in Athribis the heart, and in Abydos the head was sacred. Nevertheless, in the same temples, in sharp logical contradiction to this cult of the separate parts, men held also by the myth of the burial of Osiris as a whole, and celebrated feasts in commemoration of it.

This belief in the mutilation of the corpse of Osiris seems to have been strongest in early times in Egypt, for it could be brought into connection with the dismembering of the human corpse which was then customary. It was divided into a varying number of pieces, but the severance of the head from the rest of the corpse was considered specially important. The pieces were buried in the cultivated land, probably near to the former dwelling of the deceased. After a time, when the flesh had decayed, they dug up the bones, collected and cleaned them, and buried them in their final tomb in the sand of the desert at the edge of the Nile Valley.

THE REALMS OF THE EGYPTIAN DEAD

Even in the age of the pyramid builders this custom had become less common, though it was not entirely forgotten in much later times. Religious formulas in funerary texts are based on the belief that the severed head will be restored to the dead man in the next world. Occasionally the custom was actually practiced even in comparatively late periods. Bodies have been found which were first beheaded; then the rest of the body was embalmed, the head fastened to the neck with a stick, and the whole swathed in mummy cloths. In the pyramid age the entire body was sometimes treated in similar fashion. It was allowed to decay, the different bones were collected, each was wrapped separately in linen, and the linen packets were placed together in the order corresponding to the position of the bones in the human skeleton.

The dismembering and reconstruction of the corpse was not, in later times at least, the result merely of a wish to facilitate the dead man's passage into the other world; side by side with that intention ran in all likelihood the hope of throwing obstacles in the way of his return into this world. In common with other peoples the ancient Egyptians regarded the dead as being bereft of all the joy of existence, and for the most part malicious beings who, filled with envy, must needs long to vex and distress their survivors. The more carefully the rites of burial were carried out the sooner might the departed souls be appeased; to satisfy them fully was difficult, if not impossible. It was therefore important to resort to the same expedients which have been employed by the peoples of many lands to protect themselves against the dead who might return to earth as vampires; e.g., cutting off the head of the corpse. Where the human body is considered the only possible form for the dead to take, this remedy might be regarded as infallible, but this was not the case in the Nile Valley, where the dead man returning to earth did not need to enter his own body again but might choose from many other forms at his disposal. There was danger of his so doing if he observed the mutilation of his body and wished to punish the perpetrators of the deed. This must have been the consideration that led the Egyptians to reconstruct the body after dismembering it. If the dead man came to his grave to see that all was right and the corpse seemed in outward appearance in perfect condition, he was satisfied. If in an unhappy moment it occurred to him to re-enter it, the body fell to pieces or lost the head, and his hope of regaining his former shape was annihilated. Such thoughts certainly assume a remarkable absence of insight on the part of the dead man. But that again is a conception common to almost all nations. Death and the devil and the spirits belonging to their circle are commonly represented as stupid and easily deceived. Countless examples of this are to be found not only in the tales of the ancient and modern East; in the folk-lore of northern nations there is rich and varied illustration of the same ideas.

Occasionally the legend of the dismemberment of the body of Osiris is associated with the similar treatment of the human corpse, but this occurs seldom in comparison with the countless number of assertions that the body of Osiris was buried intact. It was his relatives who fulfilled this pious duty, and thus showed men what it became them to do in similar cases. Isis sang the lament over her brother, supported by their sister Nephthys, and repeated the spells which would protect the dead against the dangers of the next world. The jackal-headed Anubis, who, like the Greek Hermes, stands ready to accompany the dead into the land of shadows, did not confine himself to this duty for Osiris, but undertook the burial also. Horus, the son of Osiris, avenged his father's death on the murderer Set, and after long and changeful conflict wrested from him the succession to the throne of Egypt.

But the great result of all this zeal on the part of the survivors was this- Osiris gained the power to go on living in his former shape, to overcome the demons of the other world, and to found a new kingdom in their dominion, over which he reigned as a gracious and just ruler of the dead even as he had once ruled in this world over the living.

The myth in this form was to the Egyptian of historic times a type of his own lot. Like Osiris he must die, but like Osiris he hoped to rise again and to live on in the world to come not only in his earthly body, but generally also with his earthly rank, as a loyal subject and vassal of his god and king. In this cycle of conceptions the embalming of the body was considered the chief requisite for securing the permanence of the personality. That elaborate treatment of the corpse which has long seemed the most striking of Egyptian customs had for its aim the hindrance of the rapid decay incident to so hot a climate.

The Egyptian method of arresting it was certainly very simple and somewhat rough. The body was first treated with natron, and thus deprived of moisture; then bitumen was poured over it to destroy the germs of decay. Wonderful as it is that corpses thus treated have resisted decay so as to have lasted centuries long down to our own time, it must be noted that the mummy has only a distant resemblance to the body which the ancient Egyptian inhabited in his lifetime. It was impossible to preserve the soft internal parts from destruction. Lungs, heart, stomach, intestines were removed at the beginning of the process, and also the brain, as being the earliest victim of decay. As the result of the mutilation of the body for this purpose the whole abdomen fell in; moreover, the bone between the nose or mouth and the cavity of the brain was destroyed that the brain might be extracted. The natron and bitumen consumed the fleshy tissues, leaving the bones and the black or dark brown skin. It is only in the case of the very carefully treated mummies of distinguished persons, especially of kings and queens, that the features remained recognizable; the corpses of the common people present, for the most part, a repulsive appearance. The corpse was laid carefully in the coffin, the mouth closed, the arms crossed on the breast or laid straight alongside the body, which was usually stretched horizontally on the back. In earlier periods there are some exceptions to this rule. In the Nagada period, before that of the pyramids, when embalming was far less common, the bodies were usually placed in a crooked position, and so they have been found as skeletons; the knees drawn up to the breast, the arms resting partly upon them and the hands placed over the face. The dead must rest in the grave in the position in which the child awaits its entrance into the world, which by further analogy was ascribed also to the soul awaiting the resurrection. Somewhat later and down to about 2000 b.c. the corpse was often placed upon the left side, or if on the back the head was turned to the left.

That was the direction- looking towards the West and the realm of the dead- in which it was believed that the dead man could see out of his coffin and step forth from it. To express this possibility more vividly, on a corresponding spot outside the coffin were painted or carved in relief two great eyes out of which the dead man's eyes might look. Inside the coffin and often also on the corresponding part of the wall of the tomb, the picture of a door indicated the same direction. But in order that the false doors might serve only for the dead man's exit and not be used by enemies to break into the grave and the coffin, prudent people supplied them with pictured bolts, carefully shot to. It is remarkable that in the innumerable texts devoted to setting forth the fate of the dead in the under-world, in all the references to the rites to be practiced at the grave and in the allusions to the fate of Osiris, no consideration is ever given to the significance which in historic times was ascribed to the preservation of the corpse. The belief that the soul could occasionally return to the body in order to go about on earth is not sufficient to explain the adoption of so costly and tedious a process as embalming. Still less adequate does it seem when we consider that the soul was not confined to the corpse for its choice of an earthly manifestation, but could adopt any one of many other forms at its disposal without making any demands on the survivors. This absence of such references indicates that originally the significance of the corpse was much greater, and that the measures for its preservation were carried on up to a time when the necessity for such measures no longer appeared so absolute.

This is one more example of what must often be noted in the valley of the Nile- namely, that primitive customs were kept up in strictly orthodox fashion, even after their original significance had been forgotten for centuries, or at least greatly weakened. Further indications unite with those just mentioned to show that in ancient Egypt there was a time when the belief reigned that the immortal in man would always be connected with his body, even after the visible life was extinct to earthly eyes. The duration of the immortal part was bound up with the preservation of the body. Thus the sarcophagus became the home of the departed out of which, as already mentioned, he could occasionally look, and from which he could rise to go about in the tomb. Consequently the Egyptians strove to make the grave, "the everlasting house," as large and habitable as possible and to put in it everything that had been a necessity to the deceased in his lifetime. Thus there were placed in the tomb furniture and utensils of all sorts for daily and occasional use, weapons for defense, writings with magic spells against demons or with entertaining contents to pass the time, male and female companions to enliven the loneliness of the grave, food and drink. The last especially were indispensable at all times, for the dead man felt hunger and thirst just as did a god or a man living on earth. If his cravings were not satisfied by offerings then he must needs slip out of his grave and try to steal food. If he did not succeed in this he fell in his despair on most repulsive expedients, ate dung and drank urine to still his gnawing hunger.

THE REALMS OF THE EGYPTIAN DEAD

How great was the anxiety regarding a like fate is shown in some formulas in the pyramid texts according to which the king could only hope to protect himself from such necessities by his magic power. The provision of food for the dead forms the essential part of the Egyptian worship of the dead, and the adoration of the gods is manifested mainly in similar care that these higher beings in the heavenly fields shall not have to suffer from any scarcity of food.

At first the needed gifts were brought to the dwellers in the other world in their actual form; real oxen and geese were sacrificed, bread and fruit were presented; sometimes also men were slain at the funeral with much elaborate ritual, so that the dead man might be followed quickly into the other world by the servants he needed. The only change made in the earthly form of the gifts was that they also were embalmed, that they might be as lasting as the dead body. Just as the mummy had not lost its earthly form in spite of the process it had undergone, so it was believed that the food suffered no diminution of its nutritious qualities through similar embalming. Real offerings were naturally very costly, hence there arose the idea of replacing them by counterfeit presentments. Small oxen and geese, loaves, and libation vases of stone or baked clay were placed in the grave. Sometimes tables for offerings were set up in it, bearing on the top, carved in relief, a plentiful choice of the most varied viands. By means of spells the dead man could change these simulacra into their originals and so dispose of them at his own convenience. This custom had the further advantage of rendering the gifts imperishable; no decay could touch them. Above all, however, human sacrifice, which was becoming inconsistent with advancing civilization, could now be dispensed with, and indeed it seems to have been practiced seldom in historic times. As a rule, there were laid with the dead in the grave little statuettes, the so-called Ushabtis, "answerers," those small figures of wood, stone or silicious earth that now abound in our museums. Originally it was intended that the dead man should wake them with a spell to till the land for him, and for this purpose they were supplied with farming implements, hoes and baskets. Besides these menservants with which one dead man was often supplied by thousands, he had occasionally, though not often, women-servants also, to form his harem in the next world. In early times a whole household establishment of figures, carved in wood, was placed in the grave- bakers, brewers, bearers of gifts, boatmen, etc.

We must add to the representations of offerings, besides those in plastic form, the scenes carved or painted on the walls of the tomb. In them the whole life of the ancient Egyptian is displayed before our eyes; farming from seedtime to harvest, baking, the slaughter and cutting up of oxen, the dressing of geese, brewing, pressing grapes for wine, the manufacture of various utensils. Then follow pictures of the pleasant pursuits of life- hunting in the swamps of the Nile, especially of the delta, for birds, fish, hippopotami; games of ball, dancing, gymnastics, harvest-homes, etc. These are not merely pictures from the former life of the dead man- who in the wall-scenes is always represented as a spectator- intended to keep vivid to the survivors the memory of his earthly career; they were also to serve a more important purpose.

The deceased could animate them by means of spells, so that the pictures would become realities; then the corn sprouted in the fields, the fire burned, and the dead man sat by and gazed at the activity going on before his eyes for his pleasure and profit. The food grown was intended for his table, the work of the servants secured him from want, the pictured scenes enabled him to enjoy the pleasures of the chase over and over again in reality and to the full. The pictured or modeled offerings to the dead were more convenient than the actual objects themselves, but, nevertheless, they involved a certain amount of expense.

THE REALMS OF THE EGYPTIAN DEAD

When once the idea had become common that it was possible by a spell to make real objects out of the representations of them, it was but a step to the thought that a more powerful spell could without such a medium cause the desired objects to be produced from nothing. The Egyptians soon took this step. The simple repetition of a certain consecration form sufficed to create the offering: "Be a royal gift brought to the god Osiris that he may give a thousand geese and a thousand loaves to the departed N.N.," is the formula, varied in expression, but in substance always the same, that covers countless stones in Egyptian graves It either stands alone or in company with longer invocation addressed to passers-by adjuring them to repeat the spell as a favor to the dead. The dedication is in the royal name, for in the Nile Valley Pharaoh was regarded as the appointed intercessor between his people and the god. He was himself of divine origin and sprang from the union of a god, usually the Sun-god Ra, with a mortal woman, generally the wife of his predecessor on the throne. As such he was certain to gain a ready hearing among the higher powers whose circle he had left only for a short time and to which he hoped to return after death as a comrade and equal. In more primitive times the ruler himself had celebrated all acts of worship among which making offerings for the dead was one of the most important. As the state developed and practical considerations prevented this many-sided activity, the prayers and offerings were still made in his name, in order to preserve and emphasize in any intercourse with the gods this ancient custom and duty.

The gift was not supposed to go direct to the dead man, but to the god, who transferred it to the proper recipient. This practice seemed to correspond to the facts of earthly life. In the valley of the Nile every man owed his position, his property, his food, to the king, who had granted to him either the things themselves or the opportunity of earning them. Even the noblest was counted in theory a vassal of Pharaoh, though he would have resisted jealously any interference of the king in his private affairs or business. As things were theoretically in this world, so they were supposed to be in the next. Here, too, the divine king was absolute lord of all his subjects, especially of the dead. He who wanted to benefit the dead proceeded most wisely when he applied to this king and begged him, out of his plenty, to allow what was offered to any particular dead man to reach the one for whom it was intended. The god could do this in two ways- either simply by a gift, or more solemnly by means of a decree which in his kingly capacity he issued to the deceased, carefully drawn up in prescribed legal form. In many tombs, especially of later periods, such decrees are preserved drawn up on papyrus or on stelae. The survivors placed them in the tomb in the hope that the god would confirm their contents at the right moment and order them to be carried out by the subject gods and the spirits of lower rank.

In these formulas the generosity of the survivors takes a peculiar development. As long as real offerings had to be brought, as long even as pictures or images seemed necessary, they had been satisfied to give little- perhaps one ox or a few loaves. But the moment it became a mere matter of words they showered gifts on the dead in thousands. The trouble was no greater, and the satisfaction of the dwellers in eternity so much surer. In repeating the spells it was important to distinguish exactly the name of him for whom the gifts were destined, for fear other less favored beings should seize the offerings and keep them back from the rightful owner. In such documents, therefore, besides a man's own name, that of his mother is generally added as a distinction, for in theory the Egyptians always held the descent from the mother to be the surer and more important. This was especially the case in all religious matters; even in times when in secular life, and above all in questions of inheritance, increased importance was attached to the descent from the father.

THE REALMS OF THE EGYPTIAN DEAD

The gifts were brought to the grave and arranged there; the spell was spoken in the grave or at its entrance. It was assumed that the dead man was present in person, and that he had taken up his abode as a permanency in his corpse. The custom survived long after the belief connected with it had faded, and people assigned to the deceased a far wider dwelling-place than that afforded by the narrow limits of the tomb. The Egyptians still strove perpetually not only to make the tomb dwelling as pleasant and comfortable as possible, they continued to treat the mummy as if it were really the immortal personality.

They placed amulets upon it to facilitate its journey into the other world, and provided it with collections of spells to be spoken there. In short, they equipped it in every possible way for the journey to the gods. And yet it was not the mummy which was to take this journey, but something else, outwardly exactly like it, but personally a wholly distinct being, distinguished by the Egyptian as the "Osiris" of the dead man. The Egyptians never tried to explain the contradiction in the conception we have described. The relation of the "Osiris" to the mummy is a fact which we can only assert and accept, however illogical the belief in two like yet unlike forms of the same personality may appear. The origin of the belief is explained by the fact that at first the mummy was considered the lasting dwelling of the immortal personality, while later it was supposed to be represented by the "Osiris." But notwithstanding the changed conceptions of the immortal part of man, the nation did not venture to give up its ancient habits and customs, although these had been made void of meaning by the new doctrines.

The journey of the "Osiris" of the dead from the tomb to the throne of Osiris the king forms a large portion of the contents of the religious writings of the Middle and New Kingdoms, that is, from about 2500 B.C.; and to this the best known and most widely diffused of these texts, namely, the so-called Book of the

THE REALMS OF THE EGYPTIAN DEAD

Dead, is devoted. It contains the spells by means of which the dead man may hope to surmount the hindrances that he meets with in the course of his journeying. Above all, as we have already noted, it contains the names of the demons of the under-world as well as the names of objects there, this knowledge being most important to the dead man, since to the Egyptian the name was not a mere chance mark of the thing it belonged to, but an essential part of it. Gods and demons must perforce favor the man who knows and can pronounce their names. According to an old legend, the goddess Isis succeeded by stratagem in compelling the Sun-god to whisper his name in her ear, and thereby appropriated the power of the divine king and became the greatest of the goddesses.

A demon could do no more mischief to a man who called him correctly by name in the under-world; if the deceased named a gate it flew open before him; if he knew the right word, the thing which corresponded to it became his. It is remarkable that the Egyptian never attempted to map out the way leading from the grave to the eternal home even in the inexact fashion in which he tried to plan out the underworld in the "Book of that which is in the Duat" or the "Book of the Gates." Not even the order was fixed in which the dead man must pass through the separate Spaces. Hence there is no fixed succession for the different sections of the Book of the Dead. One thing only seems sure- the way traverses the earth. Sometimes the dead man walks, sometimes he goes by boat; in fact, he travels just as he might in his lifetime have traveled in the Delta. The beasts of prey that threaten him are those of earth, such as snakes and crocodiles. He longs for food; he longs even more for drink, and early in his journey a goddess hands him drink from a tree, just as in the desert it is among trees that the earthly wanderer finds life-giving water. The direction of his journey is towards the west, where the sun sets, and where behind desolate wastes the secret of the land of the blessed is hidden.

THE REALMS OF THE EGYPTIAN DEAD

Occasionally in these representations the north, or the sky near the Great Bear, appears as the abode of the dead, side by side with the kingdom of Osiris in the west. Here we have interpolated into the midst of Osirian doctrines conceptions in origin altogether different, and placing the land of the dead in the sunless north. In the Osirian teachings the land of the west is synonymous with the land of the dead, and in this belief the dead were buried on the west side of the Nile Valley, on the edge of the desert through which they had to take their way. It is needless here to picture the separate incidents of the journey, regarding which opinions have varied not only in different times, but even in the same period. It ended in the Hall of the Double Truth, in which Osiris, supported by forty-two attendants, sat as judge of the dead.

The jackal-headed Anubis led the dead man into the hall, where he uttered a long prayer in which he enumerated forty-two sins of which he was not guilty. He had wronged no man, had not oppressed his fellows, had been guilty of no malice, had committed no deed abhorrent to the gods, had not led masters to do injury to their slaves, had caused no one to suffer hunger or to weep, had neither committed nor commanded a murder, had not destroyed nor taken from the sacrificial bread, had not stolen the clothes and swathings of the dead, had been guilty of no immoral act, etc. At the end of this appeal the truth of the assertions was tested by Thoth, god of wisdom and writing, and Horus, son of Osiris. They weighed the heart of the dead man against the symbol of Truth, and sentence was pronounced according to the result. The Book of the Dead says little as to the fate of him who failed to satisfy the test. It speaks of his punishment, of his destruction, of the threatening Devourer from the Land of the West, but no details are given.

The possessor of a copy of the Book of the Dead hoped by his knowledge of magic to escape this terrible fate, and he needed no description of it. That lot only was pictured which each man desired for himself- the dwelling in the realm of the just, the justified, in the Fields of Aalu. This realm was figured after the likeness of earth, and closely resembled the delta even in its name, "Aalu" meaning in the first place the plants that spring up in swampy ground. Through it flowed a Nile, which with its wide-spreading branches formed islands, where dwelt the dead and the gods. Here the immortals ate and drank, fought with their enemies, hunted, amused themselves playing draughts either with their companions or with their own soul, sacrificed to the gods, sailed about on the canals. Their chief employment was agriculture, the various processes of which are exactly depicted in representations of the Fields of Aalu. First the soil is turned up with the plow, then the seed is sown; afterwards the corn, which has grown much above a man's height, is reaped with a sickle; oxen tread out the grain from which the chaff is winnowed and which at last is offered up to the god of the Nile, to whom is primarily due the blessing of harvest.

This doctrine- a comparatively simple one, and conceiving the life after death as much the same as life on earth- is certainly one of the oldest theories of immortality held by the Egyptians.

Similar conceptions have been found among the most various nations. According to the primitive form of this doctrine each man kept the position which he had held on earth; he who had ruled in Egypt remained forever a ruler; he who had served was ever a servant. Gradually, however, the wish crept in to prepare for the dead a happier lot than he had enjoyed on earth. This end was to be gained by means of spells which would enable him to lead a free and joyous life in the Fields of Aalu, served by the Ushabti statuettes that his friends had placed in his tomb. Should this celestial life pall, he could return to wander about on earth visiting the places that had been dear to him, or could sojourn for a season in his grave and there receive the offerings of his friends. Or he could change himself into a heron, a swallow, a snake, a crocodile, a god, could indeed take any form that he pleased. This re-incarnation at pleasure is not the Indian doctrine of transmigration; it was not intended to bring about a gradual purification of the soul but was a privilege falling to the lot of the dead who were pronounced just, who were well versed in the necessary magic spells. It procured for such an one the greatest possible mobility, the greatest strength imaginable; it equipped him with all-penetrating power and allowed him from time to time to pervade everything and all things, without, however, being merged in the All or losing any part of his individuality.

Side by side with the conception of the dead as traveling in person to the West, there was from earliest times another and much more complicated conception, contradictory of the first and unreconciled with it. According to this the immortal part- which together with the body buried as a mummy had formed the earthly man- was not a homogeneous being as most races have assumed, but was composed of various elements. These separate parts, the number of which varied greatly according to different dogmas, were united in the body, but at the moment of death they left it, and each alone sought its way into eternity. This doctrine was grafted on to the more common one of the Fields of Aalu by supposing that after the judgment scene the various parts of the dead man were allowed to come together again, so that the earthly being existed once more in flesh, blood, and soul, and would henceforth dwell in the land of the blessed. Usually, however, these parts of the soul are treated in the texts as entirely independent beings, and they play such an important part in Egyptian conceptions of the other world that we must here consider briefly at least the chief of them.

The best known part of the soul is the "Ka," a form

exactly resembling the man, born with him and remaining with him till he dies. But as regards the king it was supposed to be somewhat otherwise. In sculptured scenes the King's Ka appears behind the monarch in the form of a little man, and sometimes the king is seen approaching his own Ka with prayers and offerings, receiving from it in return promises of success, fortune and power. A corresponding relationship between themselves and their Kas was doubtless attributed to the gods, each of whom possessed his own Ka. The great temple of Memphis, for example, is not known merely as the dwelling of the god Ptah, but is distinguished also as the "Fortress of the Ka of Ptah." In the moment of death the Ka left the man, becoming itself henceforth his real personality. To the Ka are addressed both prayers and offerings, for it needed food and drink, and dwelt in eternity without losing the power to return occasionally to the grave, to become "the Ka living in the coffin" and to remain for a time united with the mummy.

The belief in this dual personality of man may well have originated in dreams. During a man's life his bodily form might sometimes be seen by his sleeping friends, he himself being far from them, and the same thing might happen after his death. It is also clear that the idea of the Ka has much in common with the idea of the "Osiris" of the dead. Here one is led to surmise that two strains of belief mingled in the conventional religion of Egypt. According to one the immortal Double is called the "Osiris," according to the other it is called the "Ka." A third figure, which seems to have closely resembled the other two, played some part in the beginning of the New Kingdom, especially in Thebes. This is the "Khou" or "Akhou," "the perfect shining one" of the dead.

Occasionally it is adored as a god; again, prayers for the dead are made to it, and, as in the fusion of two originally separate ideas the Egyptian could speak of the Ka of the Osiris of the immortalized dead, so he could invoke also the Ka of his Khou.

The name of a man calls up the mental image of him, and that this experience affected the belief in the Ka, and may, indeed, have given rise to it, is indicated by the fact that occasionally Ka and Name are put on the same level. Attention has already been called to the importance of the Name, which is sometimes regarded as an immortal part of the man possessing an independent personality. Another part of the soul, the "Ba," or human-headed bird, could, as we have seen, be considered the soul of the man. It is often represented visiting the mummy, caressing it with its human hands or going down into the grave to refresh it with food and drink. There are three other independent souls of which mention is made in the texts. The "Sahu" has the form of a man swathed in mummy cloths. The "Khaibit," usually represented as a huge fan, is really intended as the shadow cast by the man in his lifetime, which, like Peter Schlemihl's Shadow in Chamisso's tale, had a real existence of its own. Finally, there is the "Sekhem," "the reverend form," an incarnation of the man's outward appearance, transfigured indeed, but nevertheless retaining its likeness to him. These three soul elements resemble the "Osiris" or the Ka so closely that it seems probable that they were adopted into the Osirian cult from other parallel creeds. It is noticeable also that though they are often named, nothing exact is known about them and no clearly defined significance is accorded them.

Much more important in the religious texts is the "Ah," the heart of the man. The heart was considered by the Egyptians to be in general the seat of life. If the dead man wished to rise and live again he must obtain possession of this absolutely indispensable organ. In connection with this idea there was developed an independent doctrine of the journeying of the heart, which was supposed to leave the man at his death to wander into the other world. Here the dead man found it and at length succeeded in uniting himself with it anew. This temporary separation of the organ of life from the body presented a great difficulty to the thoughtful Egyptian. Without the heart life was impossible to the body and therefore impossible also to the "Osiris," which was pictured as identical in form with the body.

To overcome this difficulty it was resolved to give the mummy an artificial heart to make up for the loss of the real one, the place of which was supplied by round flints of a reddish brown color, or later by little models of the vessel in which the heart was placed when taken out of the body at the embalming. Sometimes it is represented by large images of the scarabaeus, flattened on the under side, the creature which, in the Nile Valley, always symbolized life and development. Having previously been animated by spells the artificial heart was inserted in the place formerly occupied by the real organ, and it was hoped that its presence would restore to the body warmth and vitality. The correct magic formula was written sometimes on the heart-scarabseus itself, sometimes in the collection of spells given for the use of the "Osiris." Other less important constituent parts of the immortal being need not here be noticed.

It is sufficiently clear from what has already been passed in review that many independent beliefs combined in producing the doctrine of immortality as set forth in the Book of the Dead and similar texts. Holding fast to all that he had inherited from his fathers, the ancient Egyptian certainly possessed a multitude of religious conceptions; a homogeneous religion he never developed. We may ask how it was possible for him at one and the same time to believe all these contradictory doctrines; to hold that after death he would dwell in the gloomy regions of the under-world, that he would travel the heavens with the sun, that he would till the ground in the fields of the blessed, that his soul would fly to heaven in the likeness of a bird, that it would wander towards the West, a complete entity in human form, and that it would be dissolved into the many parts of its immortal personality. The question cannot be answered. Modern research can only establish the fact that all these conceptions were co-existent and regarded as equally authoritative. This it is constrained to do even at the risk of placing in a less favorable light- at any rate as regards the realm of speculative religious thought- that "wisdom of the Egyptians" so highly extolled by classical authors. As exhibited in their own records the creed of the Egyptians as to the life beyond death presents an extraordinary medley of philosophic notions and the crudest ways of thinking belonging to primitive and uncultured peoples.

BIBLIOGRAPHIC APPENDIX

Like the beliefs of other nations as to life after death, Egyptian eschatology was bound up with. Egyptian religion, being the outcome of beliefs as to the nature of the world and man. No consecutive history of Egyptian religion has yet been attempted.

For a brief general summary of the main features of Egyptian religion and Egyptian beliefs as to the nature of life after death, see articles by F. Ll. Griffith in the Special Courses Magazine of the National Home-Reading Union, 1898, 1899, on Religion, The Disposal of the Dead, The Funeral Ritual and the Funerary Texts, The Book of the Dead.

The principal exponent of the whole subject is M. Maspero, who has given a full popular account of his views in chaps, i. ii. of his *Histoire Ancienne des Peuples de l'Orient Classique*, tome x. Les Origines (English edition, Dawn of Civilization, 1894, price 24s.). For the researches which led him to these views, see his *Etudes de Mythologie et d'Archeologie Egyptiennes* (Paris, 1893; price 20.s). He holds that the Egyptians were essentially polytheistic.

Wiedemann, in his *Die Religion der Alten Aegypter* emphasizes above all the incoherence, contradictions and conservative syncretism of Egyptian religion: "Avoiding any attempt to interpret or to systematise, I have endeavored to set before the reader the principal deities, myths, religious ideas and doctrines as they are to be found in the texts." The quotation is from the preface to an English edition (1897), revised and augmented by the author, with illustrations and full index (price is 6d.).

A paper, by the same author, on the Ancient Egyptian

THE REALMS OF THE EGYPTIAN DEAD

Doctrine of Immortality was also amplified for an English edition (1895). This little book (price 5s) which is illustrated, is an interesting introduction to the subject.

Religion and Conscience in Ancient Egypt, by Prof. Petrie, is, especially in the first part, a brilliant and suggestive generalization. The author regards national religions as in origin essentially tribal or racial, and the presence of heterogeneous and contradictory elements as evidence of fusion of races. Applying this key to Egyptian religion, he finds magic to represent the religious stratum of the indigenous (negro?) population, the Osirian cult to be mainly Libyan, the cosmic or solar worship centering in Heliopolis to be Mesopotamian, the worship of personified qualities to have been imposed by the dynastic ("Puntite") race- all fused together in prehistoric times (London, 1898; price 2s. 6d.).

Erman, the founder of the historical treatment of the Egyptian language, writing in 1885, considered it as then impossible to give a satisfactory scientific account of the religion. He presented the subject, however, in chaps, xii. xiii. of his *Aegypten* (English edition, Life in Ancient Egypt, published 1894; price 21s. net), and whatever he says as to the sacred writings is of great weight. His latest conclusions will probably be found in the forthcoming Handbook to the Religious Papyri in the Berlin Museum.

Brugsch, *Die Religion und Mythologie der Alien Aegypter*, Part I. 1884, Part II. 1888 (16s.). It is a serious undertaking to read the 750 pages of this book, of which there is no English translation. The writer contends that the Egyptian religion was throughout monumental times everywhere one and the same, essentially an exalted monotheism; but the texts he quotes in support of his view are mostly of Ptolemaic date. The value of the book lies in data of the Graeco-Roman period, but these are very unsafe guides in studying the religion of earlier epochs.

One of the first Egyptologists to give a general view of the Egyptian religion, Le Page Renouf, in his *Origin and Growth of Religion as illustrated by the Religion of Ancient Egypt* (Hibbert Lectures, 1879; 10s 16d.), contended that the Egyptian religion was originally pure and monotheistic, though afterwards debased by accretion of mythology.

Lanzone's *Dizinario di Mitologia Aegizia* gives the Egyptian deities in the alphabetical order of their names together with their figures, titles, definitions of the roles attributed to them, and references to the principal texts relating to them (Turin, 1881-6; price 11 Lira).

Maspero, in *Les Inscriptions des Pyramides de Saggarah* (1894; 3 Lira 5s.) published the Pyramid texts for the first time, he giving them in hieroglyphic and in translation. The originals are inscribed in the pyramids of five consecutive kings of the fifth and sixth dynasties. These are the oldest collections of Egyptian religious texts known, and correspondingly important.

Several English translations have been made of the body of texts known as The Book of the Dead; the latest and most popular of these is that by Dr. Budge (Kegan Paul, 1898; 3 vols., price 2 pounds, 10s.).

P. 21. "The Book of that which is in the Under-world." The abridged version from originals on papyrus, text and translation, with illustrations, see *Le Livre de ce qu'il a dans l'hades* by G. Jequier (Paris, 1894; price 8s.).

"The Book of the Gates." The text- without translation-

and its Egyptian illustrations on the sarcophagus of Sety I. (Sloane Museum, London) is given in The Sarcophagus of Oimenepthah by Bonomi and Sharpe (Longmans, 1864; out of print). For a study of these texts, see Maspero's *Les Hypogees royaux de Thebes* in his *Etudes de Religion et de Mythologie Egyptiennes.*

For the Funeral Ritual, see plates, text and translation into Italian, *Il Libro dei Funerali*, Schiaparelli (Turin, 1881-1890); Maspero, *Le Rituel du Sacrifice Funerarie* in his *Etudes*; and *La Table d'Offrandes* in *Revue de l'Histoire des Religions*, 1897.

Students wishing to investigate the original sources for themselves will find the needful guidance to publications of texts, scenes of ritual, &c, and to the general archaeology of the subject, in the footnotes and references of the works named in the above list. Before building any theories on these documents a student should carefully note the testimony of scholars as to the difficulty of reading, let alone interpreting them. (See, e.g., Erman, *Life in Ancient Egypt* pp. 343 et seq. and Griffith in The Book of the Dead, National Home-Reading Union Special Courses Magazine.) Theories founded on the authority of Herodotus, Plutarch, Diodorus, etc, are to be regarded with great caution, not only because these writers lived at a late and decadent period in Egyptian history, but also because of their credulity, and their imperfect equipment for observing and recording the manners and customs of a foreign people. All the valuable indications to be gathered from their statements require careful checking from Egyptian sources, literary and archaeological. (On this point, see Griffith, pp. 162 el seq. of *Authority and Archaeology, Sacred and Profane*, edited by D. G. Hogarth; Murray, 1899; price 16s.)

THE END

31951077R00026

Made in the USA
Lexington, KY
26 February 2019